WITH THE
33rd "Q.V.O." LIGHT CAVALRY

IN MESOPOTAMIA

The Naval & Military Press Ltd

Published by
The Naval & Military Press Ltd
5 Riverside, Brambleside, Bellbrook
Industrial Estate, Uckfield, East Sussex,
TN22 1QQ England
Tel: +44 (0) 1825 749494
Fax: +44 (0) 1825 765701
www.naval-military-press.com
www.military-genealogy.com

In reprinting in facsimile from the original, any imperfections are inevitably reproduced and the quality may fall short of modern type and cartographic standards.

PREFACE.

This small volume has been compiled by me, from the diaries of my brother, the late Major M. H. Anderson, 33rd "Queen Victoria's Own" Light Cavalry, and from extracts of his letters to me, written while he was on service with his regiment in Mesopotamia. It covers a period from the 8th November 1914, the day he sailed from India, to the 29th April 1915, the day on which he was killed in action.

A few extracts from daily papers, etc., which are of interest have also been inserted. From the above, it will be seen that the contents of the following pages are an account of his personal experiences and views, and as such may be of some interest, and in consequence I have had them printed.

This book is only for private circulation, and is not for sale.

E. S. J. ANDERSON.

QUETTA,
October 1915.

WITH THE 33rd "Q.V.O." LIGHT CAVALRY IN MESOPOTAMIA.

November 8th. Embarked on "Ellora." Ship not ready, so some delay, but all on board 3-30 p.m. Awfully hot; syce nearly left behind; out of dock at 6 p.m. and sailed.

November 9th. Exercised horses in afternoon, grooming and allowing men to get accustomed to their surroundings, during the morning. Very nice ship and cool for horses, and most comfortable for us (officers). My apartments sumptuous, Captain very pleasant. Lovely day.

November 10th. Beautiful day. Exercised all the horses, morning, rifle and sword inspection, and "A" squadron exercise at 4. Men settling down, and things getting straight.

November 11th. Land in sight at breakfast.

November 12th. Sharp storm, lasted about an hour.

November 13th. Reached Fao, at least the bar, about 11 a.m. Naval Officers came along with pilot about 11; owing to swell some delay in getting on board.

November 14th. Crossed the bar about 6-30, and reached Abaddan about 11, anchored just above the oil mills. Country flat and desert, except one mile from the banks date groves.

November 15th. Only landed thirty-six horses (two barges), could get no others, hope for more to-morrow. Watched action at bend of river and shells bursting.

November 16th. Started unloading horses early; great delays in getting barges, no more available, eighty horses still on board. Went off to staff, and promised to disembark all if barges and tugs provided. Got the last lot after dinner; one horse appeared to have gone mad, became alright. Eventually all on shore at 10 p.m. Received operation orders. Searchlight going all night.

November 17th. One squadron advance guard, Dickson, Massy, and self; Grantham main body.

November 18th. No entry.

November 19th. One squadron with Massy and Grantham reconnaissance to Balzaniah. Visited E's camp first, found all ammunition not burnt had been looted; my bonfire of fifteen boxes had burnt successfully. G. with patrol, I supporting, M. with main body, all went well, and connection successfully kept. Interpreter much wanted when talking with villagers, all seemed most friendly at Balzaniah. Great caution taken, but suddenly patrol fired on at close quarters, *i.e.*, three hundred yards, two horses fell, and G. turned to help. This I saw and then mounted troop to assist, thinking them wounded; having proceeded some way saw them,—great relief.—Naval action going on on our left from 12 to 3; from the smoke one of their ships burned. Cut two wires, gathered lucern on way back to camp, 4-15. G.O.C. pleased with report. Quarter rations.

November 20th. Massy and one troop escort Intelligence Officer towards Balzaniah. Dickson and two troops cut lucern, got full rations. Dickson to get stores from ship, back in time for parade reconnaissance.

November 21st. Balzaniah again, and towards Abdul Kasib found no enemy, and reported all gone North and Basra. Four abandoned guns reported, visited them on island in newly-made embrasures, field guns and carriages all left and some shells. Interesting day. Back at 3. Orders to march at 8, marched all night, pace dreadfully slow after midnight, frequent long halts while road was prepared. Halted at 9, as still fourteen miles off; reached Basra about 12. Transport began to come in about 4. On march, water a difficulty.

November 22nd. State entry arrangements made. Our camp not well situated, proposed new camp found to be an inhabited village, so returned to our old camp.

November 23rd. Busy. Despatched patrol to look for missing man of 117th, failed to find him, but brought in one horse of "A" squadron with blanket on. Arabs brought in two more from Zoubair direction. State entry, somewhat cramped for room, only those close by could hear the proclamation.

November 24th. Began to rain at dinner time, and did so most of the evening. Massy left with five men to get our heavy kit left on the "Ellora."

November 25th. Everything wet. Rendezvous three miles, with three troops to Zoubair, going awfully deep mud, very cold wind, had to walk to pillar about nine miles, and then going good. Sheikh with us, gave us (a) splendid lunch, and to men and horses; wonderfully clean town full of well-to-do Arabs, merchants to Bombay, Delhi, etc. Going better returning. Heard of two horses at Fao.

November 26th. Visited our new camp. Dirt and refuse indescribable; two troops under Grantham to help collect arms from village one mile off near Zoubair Gate. Six horses still missing, lucky so few, both mine caught; black; rope galls, bay; nil. Twenty-seven with galls out of eighty-six stampeded.

November 27th. Two troops under Dickson to Shaiba. Ram Karan and one troop to look for horses on road to Abdul Kasib, found none. Bhim Khan and one troop to complete collection of arms. Moved to new camp; took two troops on to complete cleaning up, also coolies helping did a good deal. A trying day pottering about. Massy returned having got all the kit, and landed it by 1-30; very good work.

November 28th. Grantham with one squadron to Abdul Kasib, a political expedition. Routine work in lines.

November 29th. No work. Church parade. Good sermon.

[The following letter was received by me from my brother, dated "Basra, 29th Nov. 15," which is more or less an account in narrative form of the contents of the Diary given above; there are, however, little incidents recorded in it, which have not been mentioned in the diary, so I think it is worth while to insert it here. It may be mentioned that this letter was opened by the Censor, but nothing was erased or obliterated.]

Extract from first letter:—

"The first day of peace that (I) have had since we left Bombay on the 8th Nov. We had a hard day's work embarking two squadrons on the 'Ellora,' an excellent B.I. boat, very comfortable and clean. I was O.C. troops, there were three S. and T. Officers on board, and a few details. We all had two cabins to ourselves, so were very comfortable indeed; the Captain a delightful man, and did everything to make us and the horses comfortable. We arrived at the entrance of the river on the 13th, and crossed the bar at daylight. The next morning with five ships anchored at Abadan, just above the oil works at 11 a.m. The country each side as flat as a billiard table, with a fringe of date palms along the river of from four hundred yards to a mile. Sunday, 15th, disembarked only thirty-six horses, as could not get barges and tugs; our arrival had been kept very secret. With great difficulty we managed to land all horses and men by 11 p.m. on Sunday 15th owing to delays in getting barges. The Poona Brigade had already had an encounter with the enemy. We could hear the guns firing, and the shrapnel bursting on the morning of the 14th, the enemy made a vigorous attack at dawn and got within thirty yards of our trenches. We received orders to advance on the 16th, one squadron, advance guard, one head of the main body. I was with the former, and our instructions were to keep about fifteen hundred yards East of the palm trees, which we did. We started at dawn, and after about two and an half hours sighted the enemy apparently retiring along the trees towards a mud fort, and some digging trenches. Massy, who was in advance sent an excellent report of their position, having seen guns, and trenches covering about one and a half (miles), he joined me, and I sent him with his report to the G.O.C. advance guard. Shortly after this, their guns opened fire on us, the first shell just missed the rear of the squadron, frightening the horses. I immediately moved at a trot, the next was about twenty yards off, and we got and kept out of range, but they sent about fifteen more in our direction. Seeing the flashes I was able to accurately report the position of the guns, and our guns soon got the range, and moved into the trees, and we could not locate them again, and ever silenced them. About an hour after this, the infantry attack commenced, the advanced guard came out West, as the enemy's line extended about half a mile South of the fort, and about one mile North of the same along the trees, apparently with the intention of making a flank attack on the enemy's main position, which was a line of trenches about half a mile South of the fort extending from the trees about fifteen hundred yards West into the plain. Although the ground is perfectly flat, these trenches were very difficult to see a thousand yards away. I was told to protect our left flank. When the flank attack was about two thousand five hundred yards away, a heavy rain storm came on, which converted the plain into a sea of mud. As could see little, I halted, and when it cleared off after about twenty minutes, the infantry seemed to have edged off towards the trees, so that there was practically only a frontal attack. Just before the rain, they again tried to shell us, but we were about eight hundred yards out of range, so we also got nearer the fort, plodding away in a sea of mud; when suddenly a tremendous fire was opened by the enemy (rifle and artillery). Our infantry were about six hundred yards off

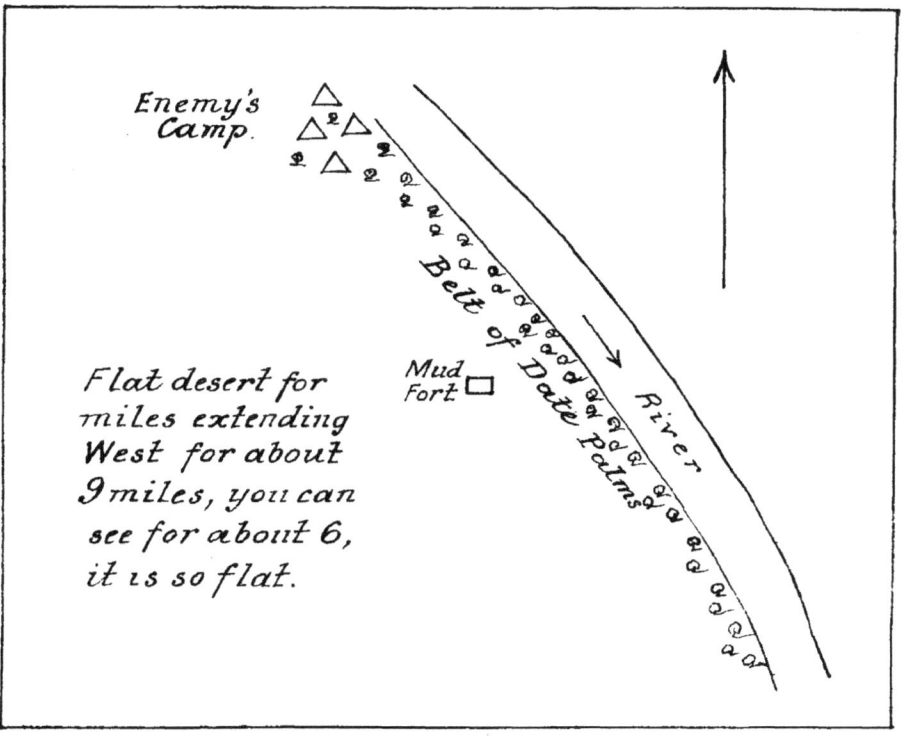

The above rough little sketch was made by my brother, and included in his first letter to me, and helps one to understand his description of the action on the 17th November 1914.

(E. S. J. A.)

their trenches, which were being shelled by our field battery and two mountain, but they remained quiet till our infantry got close. The shells and bullets fairly flew all round us. Two shells buried themselves in the mound Dickson and I were on, not ten yards off; how no man or horse was hit was wonderful. This lasted for forty minutes, when as could do nothing where we were, thought better try to work round their flank, so moved off, and Grantham joined me with the other squadron; having gone half a mile, a well directed shell (shrapnel) burst just over me, and caught the end of the squadron, slightly wounding two horses and two men; one of the horses was mine,—'Attala'—a bullet in the back, but is now alright. The case of the shell fell just in front of 'Amethyst,'* not three yards away, making her shy violently. Several shells fell fairly close, but no further damage. The going was so heavy that we had to give up the flank movement, as to bring it off had several more miles to go, so retraced our steps, and took up position on the flank of the field battery; the enemy fired spasmodically, but no shells fell near us. Having captured their camp (our infantry), about 4 orders came to go to camp, to reach which we had to cross the enemy's trenches; we saw about 60 of them dead and a proportion of wounded; of course the horses got no fodder that day. On 18th. We (two squadrons) searched for wounded, and completed burning the enemy's camp; we fired at some Arabs, who were looting it. 19th Reconnoitring, Grantham, with a patrol had a narrow escape. I was supporting him with one squadron; he was suddenly fired on from some trees about 300 yards away, and two of his patrol fell at a ditch, he turned to help them, and fortunately the enemy stopped firing, I presume thinking they had hit them, and did not recommence firing till they had mounted, and were away. I saw them fall, but did not see them remount, and was afraid they were hit and had mounted to help, when we saw them all right,—greatly to my relief—only a sword lost, which was recovered the next day. 21st Reconnoitring, with the other squadron, had a local interpreter with us,—an interesting day—found the enemy had gone, and found two guns deserted, and visited their camp, had to cross in a boat a creek, on boat Dickson, and I and two Arabs and two men as escort; we gave our informer £1. I forgot to say on the 19th a naval battle was in progress quite close to us, the enemy's guns not more than a mile away, but hidden by the trees. General Barrett personally thanked me for the very excellent information received

---

* The name of my brother's charger.

on the 17th (day of battle), and two days later put in orders that the cavalry had made a very useful reconnaissance. On the 21st we returned from reconnaisance at 3 p.m., and received orders for one squadron to march at 8 p.m., the division going to do a forced march (to) Basra. I left Dickson with the squadron that was to remain behind. We marched at a snail's pace all night, halted an hour at 9 p.m., and we reached Basra at about 12. Nothing again for the horses, but managed to buy some lucern and bhoosa; some of the infantry did not get in till 3 a.m., but really stood it wonderfully—a very trying march—and should be sorry to repeat it. The transport animals did not get in till 4 a.m., at the earliest. 23rd. State entry into Basra, proclamation, and flag raised. 24th. Rained at night most disagreeable, and on 25th, with one squadron to ZOUBAIR, 12 miles away, in a sea of mud, a wonderfully clean village; the Sheikh gave us an excellent lunch (had a political with us), and fed all the men and horses. Chiefly inhabited by Arab merchants from India. On the 22nd the squadron under Dickson left at last camp stampeded at midnight, eighty-six of them. Two cats fighting did it. We have now caught all but two, none so far badly damaged. Massy off to-morrow to bring six from a place called Fao, sixty miles from here. This is a most horrible place, all stinks and swamps, entirely devoted to date palm growing. The Turks are reported gone to Baghdad. I hear a small force pushes up the river about forty miles from here on Thursday (3rd December.) The rest of the regiment is on the river somewhere, and they probably remain on board some days, as means for disembarking are inadequate. Big steamers can come up here but no further. We have had no letters, and little news; heard of Lord Roberts' death, and loss of the 'Bulwark,'—a submarine, I suppose, horrid things.

"P.S.—The Dorsets lost thirty-three killed on the 17th. Birdwood (Political) and Twiss (R.E.) killed. I knew both. Total casualties that day three hundred and forty."

[*N.B.*—This action is, I believe, generally known as the Battle of Sahil. E.S.J.A.]

November 30th. No patrols. Routine work, rations, and men cleaning kit. Rifle inspection. Arranged for steamer for Massy to go to Fao, to fetch 6 missing horses. Our Head Quarters and other two squadrons in the river.

December 1st. One squadron escort to G.O.C. to Shaiba, Dickson and self. Very cool day. Strong cold wind at Shaiba. Deadly spot,

4 or 5 summer residences in midst of desert, about 8 miles out. G.O.C. came back very fast, had a deal of galloping to keep up. Massy left for Fao for stray horses.

December 2nd. Nothing particular.

December 3rd. Exercise, Dickson to rations. Grantham preparing to go to Shaiba with two troops. I drew seven days' rations for him. C.O., Collins, and Willoughby arrived with 49 horses with Massy. Mail in, the first since left India. Good home letters.

December 4th. Exercise and usual work. Grantham and half "C" squadron to Shaiba.

December 5th. Exercise. Took C.O. and Collins *via* Magil Road to Zoubair Gate. Usual work.

December 6th. On duty, exercise and rations.

December 7th. Exercise, and erecting screens for horses from N.W. wind.

Extract from 2nd letter, dated 7th Dec. 1914: "I cannot say where I am as it is forbidden; am wondering if my last letter reached you. Anyway we have not moved, and there appears little chance of doing so. The country is very unsuitable for cavalry, and there seems great difficulty in getting any fodder or grain, except what is imported, so fancy are stuck here. There was a fight about 40 miles North two days ago, and we took two guns, and some prisoners.

"Reinforcements were sent up the next day, as hear the enemy have been also reinforced. They made a (half-hearted) attack on our camp there yesterday, but did not get very close and retired.

"I expect all Officers in British and Indian Regiments will be dressed exactly like their men from now, as was the case in South Africa,—(very surprised to read about De Wet)—as we are now fighting at such much closer ranges, makes it all the more necessary.

"It has been quite cold with a North wind, got warmer with clouds about, a little rain yesterday, but clear and cold again. We have caught all but 4 of the 86 horses, which stampeded one night, and two are known to be in vicinity of one town, so hope to get them soon. Lucky to get so many back, and practically no damage done, beyond a few cuts and bruises.

"The papers are interesting, we get Reuters here occasionally and nothing else. 'Attala'—[one of my brother's chargers]—behaved like a fiend to-day, would do nothing but run backwards, and thought was going into the canal, so got off hastily, and gave him a thrashing. He is an awful sweep."

Diary continued:—

December 8th. Exercise with Willoughby. Orders to embark three troops for Qurna. Embarked at 4, finished at 6 p.m.

December 9th. Arrived early at Mezera, 4 miles from Qurna, disembarked at dawn. Reached camp (a burnt village) about 8 a.m. Had breakfast with G.O.C. who with Staff shortly afterwards went off to take over Qurna, one thousand and ten prisoners, and five guns. Visited battlefield, saw twenty-three unburied Turks.

December 10th. Reconnoitred to Ratta Canàl. Willoughby got a ducking trying to cross; country quite open and dry. Collins went up canal four miles, very swampy further up; only crossing from Tigris for half mile, banks fairly good, and then swampy, about 35 yards wide and 10 feet deep. Back by 4 p.m. Looked very threatening and rained a little about 7. An Arab reported Turks lost 250, including many drowned trying to re-embark, and eight hundred Turks and four thousand Arabs retired.

December 11th. Willoughby none the worse. Crossed Qurna to see Staff.

December 12th. Crossed to right bank of Tigris, did not take long, had a bath on the steamer.

December 13th. Reconnoitred right bank of Tigris, just South of Ratta Canal, saw nothing. Arabs told us enemy retired from El Ozier. Willoughby and party to fetch fodder from barge. Bitterly cold, had to run about to keep warm during dinner.

December 14th. Reconnoitred left bank Euphrates about 9 miles, swampy and intersected by creeks, some dry, difficult country for troops. Sand dunes about one mile from where river bends sharp South. Arabs very communicative: a very picturesque one, evidently the head (man), came and talked from village close by. Back by 4 p.m. Velt fires only two mile away, fine sight.

December 15th. Sir A. Barrett and Staff to inspect, as pleasant as usual. Rode with Collins to Qurna, he and W. and Sikhs to return to Basra.

Extract from 3rd letter, dated "Qurna 15-12-1914":—

"You will see from the address that have moved; this place is the junction of the Euphrates and Tigris. About a week ago two battalions were sent up here with two sections R.F.A., thinking there were three hundred Turks. They found a great many more in a strong position with guns, but drove them back the first day, took two guns, but found it advisable to retire to old camp, and ask for reinforcements. Casualties on our side about seventy. The rest of the brigade came up, and one mountain battery. Though cavalry were asked for, there was no ship to take them, as ascertained from the authorities, so none could be sent. Fought the next day, drove the enemy back, and many escaped, as could not pursue them. One thousand and ten capitulated in Qurna, as we crossed the river above the place, and caught them, also five guns.

"We have been out reconnoitring three days up each bank of the Tigris and left bank Euphrates. No one knows yet if we are to advance further, but politicals want us to go as far as Amara, about sixty-five miles from here, where the Turks have retired to; they first went back to Ezra's Tomb about sixteen miles from here. We hope that as they have not been pursued that they will return to Ezra's Tomb, and we can go and mop them up. The rest of my squadron is being sent up here and another squadron, so that if there is anything we shall be in it, but unless they make up their minds quick, the floods will any make advance impossible. The telegrams to-day are splendid: all the German cruisers abroad accounted for, and twenty thousand captured on the Yser, and seventy guns— almost the first substantial success we have had our advance after the retreat from Mons. The country up here is much more fertile than round Basra, and most of the country is covered with high reeds, which the Arabs are now burning, and one sees velt fires on all sides for miles; yesterday they were close here (two miles off) and quite a sight. The current of the Tigris is very swift, it is difficult for a boat to row against it; as the country is so flat it is rather surprising. If no advance is going to be made from here, it will be deadly, as there is nothing to do. One hopes against hope we are only here for the winter, and then on to France, as this is really the most beastly country have ever seen, absolutely flat and up to this place a fringe of date trees along the river, but beyond here even these stop. I expect to-morrow we shall reconnoitre to Ezra's Tomb. The weather is very variable, two nights ago it was very cold indeed, and had to walk about during dinner to keep warm, but last night was warmer many degrees. We brought up no tents here, but expect them soon, and shall be glad of them as it looks working up for rain, and fear will come before the tents can. Have had only one batch of letters: the post office is doing us very badly, one can't imagine why with this river as communication.

"The mosquitos here are very large and hungry,—they even attack the horses. General Barrett with staff came up here this morning to inspect and returns to Basra this evening. The days are short and the nights long, as having no tents it is too cold to sit up, and one has got to go to bed early about 8 p m., also have nothing to read except one weekly 'Times' I brought with me, as we were told were to be away for two days only. Wishing you a happy Xmas."

Diary continued:—

December 16th. W. and C. off at 10. Re-marked out camp for full squadron. Some tents and kit arrived and got it off, and tents pitched, also fifty-four blankets; men more comfortable.

December 17th. Cleaning up camp and marking out. Parade at 10-45 till 12-30. Hear enemy returned El Ozier to reconnoitre to-morrow. 1½ squadrons reported coming to-morrow morning.

December 18th. Dickson, Willoughby, and Onslow arrived, only three troops of "C." Very glad to get men's tents and kits, and replacements. Went towards El Ozier. Cramer Roberts (Norfolks) came too, got about twelve miles, and then held up by marsh land and creek. Saw good boar. One troop of "C" to left bank, Willoughby showed them the ground.

December 19th. To Baharan with Captain of Norfolks to select ground for camp of Brigade.

December 20th. Out to Baharan to see Sheikh, and get information; went without interpreter to learn better.

Extract from 4th letter, dated 20th December 1914:—

"One has really very little time, though one is doing no fighting, except in the evening, and till to-day (we have just built a mess house) it has been too cold to sit up, and one has been forced to go to bed to keep warm. As it has been in the papers, I am mentioning names of places. We are now at Qurna, that is, two squadrons under self. I don't think any real advance will be made from here, as the season is too advanced, and in a month the country commences to flood. The only way to carry on war here is with ten or fifteen flat-bottomed steamers so that you can advance rapidly, and land your troops where you want.

"We got our tents three days ago, and very glad to get them too. I have still four horses missing from the stampede, and fear they are lost altogether, either stolen or drowned in some muddy creek. I still hope this show will be over to enable us to get France about April. Tatum killed in East Africa, had the next cot to me on the 'Dongola;' a very cheery fellow."

Diary continued :—

December 21st. Sniped, very unpleasant. Bullet through Willoughby's tent. Out to see Sheikh again, gave a good deal of information. Rained about ten fairly steadily, place a quagmire, fine about 3. Lovely afternoon.

December 22nd. No sniping, quiet day, riding school and cleaning kits.

December 23rd. Sniped at night. The Arabs came quite close in, and took away some flags and screens. Took squadrons to try and find where they retired to, impossible country, high reeds, creeks, and marsh. Began to dig cover for the horses.

December 24th. Sniping, one horse shot, and died during afternoon. Two men of "C" squadron killed on patrol duty. Very busy digging trenches all the afternoon, and putting up barbed wire fence. Out looking for traces of snipers, collected about two hundred rounds and one M. H. rifle; all the men bolted on our approach.

December 25th. Went to small village again, rapid approach, so found three men and saw five bolting. Water much higher, so reeds would not burn near village. Made splendid bonfire on the way home, for about three miles, unfortunately wind wrong way. "At-home" on H. M. S. "Lawrence" at 4, talked to Colonel Peebles, Norfolks. Women of Bombay sent us an excellent plum pudding. No sniping, a great relief. "A" 2 to left bank of Tigris. "C" 4 returned.

December 26th. Rode with Willoughby to first creek, flooded. Busy all day.

December 27th. Gave the men a day off.

Extract from fifth letter, dated 27th Dec. 1914:—"It is most annoying; one cannot write in the evening, as hands and feet get so cold, so to bed one has to go. They say next month here it gets much colder. Wah! We have been hard at work building embankments to protect the horses from snipers at night. Two nights had none and last night they (the snipers) began again, but only one picquet some two thousand yards off, so none of the bullets reached us. On 24th we had one horse killed, and on 22nd an Indian Officer of the 7th Rajputs, and one battery horse killed, and one R.A. man and two mules wounded, the bullets fairly whistling about our tents—most unpleasant. On 23rd they (the enemy) came right close in, and took some flags amidst screams of joy, and the next night emboldened, got amongst the 48th Pioneers, and wounded several, *i.e.*, four with knives, but got more than they gave, as several bayonets were covered with blood to the hilt, and one deader left behind.

"I have no wish to be either shot or stuck in the dark.

"We had two men killed on patrol; they were a standing patrol and foolishly occupied the same mound daily. The Arabs marked this, and twelve at night dug a deep hole completely concealing them; the patrol came along, the scouts passed the mound at about one hundred and fifty yards each side, saw nothing, and signalled all clear, and returned to the mound. Just as they were about to dismount, a volley : both fell dead, the rest (three) had approached to about an hundred yards, were also fired on but escaped. One (man) went for reinforcements from camp five miles away, the remaining two caught two horses of the dead men, one held them, while the third kept the enemy in sight. He tried to fire, but the horse jerked his arm each time; unfortunate that they could not have bagged some of them, as the Arabs were lost in the marsh and reeds before the troop could come up. It was unfortunate, but I think the patrol acted well, if they had only bagged a few of them might have got something, as the G.O.C. expressed his approbation. On the 25th had a great bonfire lighted, about three miles of tall reeds and grass. It was a fine sight, the largest fire I have lighted, and now one can see for a long way, and ride three miles from camp without being afraid of snipers in grass. We have rather a snug mess, made of matting and reeds, it keeps out the wind and some of the rain. I have good fortifications round my tent, earth entrenchments, sandbags, and bhoosa bales; most of the men have dug holes inside their tents. The country is rapidly flooding from the Euphrates, and we soon shall be unable to move anywhere, one wonders what they will do with us, as where we now are in a month, is, I believe, all flood. Post off."

Diary continued :—

December 28th. Squadron drill, busy as usual.

December 29th. Reconnoitred to Mazeeblah. Willoughby and Onslow started first at 6-45, and had to wait owing to mist rising. Dickson and I at 10, found Willoughby one mile North of Baharan, went with him to Mazeeblah. W. and O. returned, I started back at 2, and about one mile from Baharan about forty Arabs came out of the reeds, and opened a fire, we were near a sand dune, and returned it, they hastily retired.

December 30th. Went out as far as Jala, covering party making roadway across marsh. Dull day, rained. Troop returned from left bank. Dry nullah near camp full to-day.

December 31st. Dull day. Operation orders countermanded. General D. went out and was fired on by Arabs.

January 1st. Started at 6-30 in command of advance guard. Willoughby engaged Arabs near creek South of Baharan, no other enemy, proceeded to Mazeeblah, from where saw Turkish camp on hill South of Sarifa, and about two regiments came out hurriedly and entrenched; if had had R.F.A. could have given entrenchers warm reception. General D. came up and saw and the force retired, reaching camp at dark. The flood has risen at least one foot since morning. We could not attack enemy owing to flood and unfordable creeks.

January 2nd. Exercise, busy with indents, etc.

January 3rd. Exercise, had day off. Rode into Qurna.

January 4th. Warmer day. Watering order. Dickson with patrol to left bank and Ratta Canal, saw twenty-seven Turkish cavalry.

January 5th. Bright, but bitterly cold wind. Dickson on "Shaitan." Sh. and Willoughby and Onslow with two troops supporting "Shaitan" by land.

Extract from 6th letter, dated 5th January 1915:—

"Had no letters at all last mail, but your welcome papers, and two batches of them; hope a new mail will come soon,—why the post is so irregular one cannot imagine. To-day bright sunshine, with a biting North wind. Our 'chupper' mess is a great comfort. When returning from a reconnaissance four days ago (I had only two troops, having sent on Willoughby with two) my trumpeter drew my attention to a body of about forty Arabs advancing out of the marshes, and a small sand dune being close (by) I intended dismounting to see if they were armed, when they saved me the trouble by opening fire, but soon retreated on our returning the compliment; they were too close the marshes for a charge. The bullets flew all about us for a minute or so, but no one or horse was hit. We made a reconnoissance in force two days later, and saw the enemy's camp about four miles away, and about fifteen from here, but could not reach them owing to swamps, and deep unbridged creeks. Tantalizing. They had apparently heard of our approach, and came out hurriedly and began to entrench in feverish haste,—rather amusing watching them.— Owing to the rapid rising of the floods we are all moving camp, and we with others cross the river, as the other side apparently does not flood in the same way as the right bank, all the floods come from the West apparently this time of year. One lives for news from Europe, which is very scarce: what is happening in E.A. after the set-back there, should like to know.

"To-day very slack, the others, *i.e.*, three, have all gone out on jobs, so I am alone. Government have not provided sufficient warm clothing: they ought to have given a warm shirt to each. Our thin khaki is not at all suited to this country at this time with its biting N.E. winds, there is consequently a fair amount of sickness."

Diary continued:—

January 6th. Busy in camp. Two troops under Dickson to left bank, saw nil. R.F.A. shelled Arabs on sand dunes at about four thousand yards about 5 p.m. Much sniping in camp, no casualties.

January 7th. In camp, busy, no steamers to take us across. R.F.A. shelled Arabs in force, pursuing one hundred of the 120th who had all swam across creek to round up a few seen. Evidently did good deal of damage, judging by their running backwards and forwards, and bolting from their trenches. No sniping.

January 8th. Four troops to left bank, we all went (four officers), Turks from Ratta Canal and village came out and fired on us. Jemadar Ghasi Ram's horse killed, Willoughby's wounded (slightly). Enemy showed up well and afforded good target, but steamer with guns on board was a long way behind.

January 9th. General Barrett arrived, and settled for us leaving one troop to cross to Muzar.

January 10th. "C" crossed the river to new camp at Muzar.

January 11th. "A" less one troop moved to Muzar. Open camp on border of burnt village. Got across in good time.

January 12th. Moved camp to inside date grove, a much better camp in every way. Willoughby to Qurna for rations, Dickson, Onslow and self reconnoitring.

January 13th. Onslow to fetch rations from barge opposite Camp Tigris. I in camp, Dickson and Willoughby reconnoitring.

January 14th. Usual reconnoitring, getting camp cleared. Dickson and self out, Onslow in camp and Willoughby to Qurna. Sharp sniping, bullets flying over our tents, enemy got close in, by blood tracks several were wounded. One Arab found in marsh with broken leg.

January 15th. Busy getting lines ready for Head Quarters. Collins reached camp 7-30 for mules. I went down at 9. Met C.O., helped in disembarking. Dickson and Onslow out reconnoitring. Some sniping, much warmer.

Extract from 7th letter, dated 15-1-1915 :—

"We crossed the river three days ago, and had to change camp the day after we crossed, always an annoying business and a great trouble, but we are undoubtedly in a much better camp now, and well protected by other units, with several highish walls to keep out bullets. They came close in two nights ago, and sniped, but by blood tracks, and several articles left behind, we evidently hit several of them badly, and got one wounded man with a broken leg. The Turks have evidently been reinforced, and their outposts are now six miles away; whether they intend coming down and attacking us I don't know, but rumour says they have appointed a new Civil Governor of Basra, and placed some troops at his disposal; if they come all the better, will save us the trouble of going after them. Qurna is being strengthened, and are opposite it on the other bank, in temporary trenches fairly 'pukka,' what are I believed called semi-permanent, so shall be ready to give any one a warm reception.

"We came under fairly heavy fire here one day, and an Indian Officer had his horse killed, and Willoughby his charger hit in the leg, very lucky only a flesh wound. It has started to blow hard, and we are going to have a foul 'Shamal,'—what rain storms are called in this country. Shall we ever get to France I wonder? Not at present at all events. We expect a mail to-day, but they are most irregular: why, one can't imagine."

Diary continued :—

January 16th. In camp, settling down and getting wall built, seemed busy all day, tired. A few shots just at conclusion of dinner. Very warm, began to rain about 9 p.m.

January 17th. Dickson and self out reconnoitring. We caught an Arab, armed, rifle, pistol and dagger, he told us enemy increasing in numbers, estimate at six to seven thousand. Think possibly half.

January 18th. In lines, enemy evidently reconnoitred our camp with about one hundred infantry, and were shelled by R.F.A.

January 19th. Out reconnoitring, Grantham and machine gun to support H.M.S. "Shaitan" up Shaweb River, could only get one and a half miles from Brick Kilns owing to marsh, and she went about two miles further.

January 20th. The Brigade, and R.F.A. and Norfolks advanced at daylight.

January 21st. In lines, visited Qurna with Dickson and Onslow. Very little progress made with the defences.

January 22nd. Usual patrols, enemy as usual. Warmer. Ordnance came and tents for followers.

Extract from 8th letter, dated 22-1-15 :—

"The diary reached me quite safely, and is just the sort I wanted, and your papers. Awfully kind of you sending comforters and socks to each man of my squadron, they will be much appreciated. I am feeling rather sad to-night seeing that Colonel Lempriere has been killed: such a charming man, was he not ? I saw him off at Port Said for Cairo the day the "Dongola" and "Somali" arrived there. Last Wednesday as the Turkish outposts had come rather close, and it was not known what was behind them, and report said two divisions,—(it is impossible for us to find out, as they hold a deep canal, and each flank is protected by a river and swamps, and flying machine or spies are the only means)—a reconnoissance was made in force. Their outposts were soon driven back from some sand dunes,—(which are about three miles from the canal, and about six or seven from here)—and across the canal, and we shelled them and their camps, three of which were within range. There were several thousand of them, and I think were taken completely by surprise as most of them fled in all directions, followed by our shells, over two thousand of which were fired. Our infantry advanced to within half a mile of the canal, and apparently saw lots to fire at,—(we could see little), but were walking in about one foot of water; they then retired. It seemed a pity not to burn their tents, camp, etc., which so close, but suppose the G.O.C. was right not to cross the canal, which would of course taken some time, and they might have had lots entrenchments, though there were two bridges, and others could soon have been made, as there were eight dhows in the canal, and putting two side by side would nearly have done it. It seemed such an opportunity to deliver a good blow, as (we) appeared to have taken them unprepared, but we hear there is to be no advance at present; so as the only object had been obtained, i.e., to find out their strength, we retired. We (cavalry) were the last to retire, and within an hour all the enemy were streaming back, the Arabs with many banners, delighted apparently at finding their things intact. We had fifty casualties, and reports place theirs between three and six hundred, also that the Arabs are returning home. They had several hundred mounted Arabs, but very few come this side of the canal. I think they suffered rather heavily. There is I fancy little chance of them attacking us; I wish they would try. Sunday, 24th: a wet, cold cheerless day, and the place a sea of mud. My squadron's turn to provide patrols, etc., so had rather a wet day. Fortunately there was no wind, or else it would have been very cold, but pottering about quite cold enough."

Diary continued:—

January 23rd. Very cloudy all day. Shot one dog, fired badly. "Amethyst" (the name of his charger) very unsteady, missed a "sitter" on foot. Dogs becoming very bad, poor things very hungry, I presume.

January 24th. Reconnoitring.

January 25th. In lines.

January 26th. Usual reconnoitring; dull, cloudy and rained. Walked to river.

January 27th. Busy in lines, range finding. Treasure Chest Officer came.

Making stands in horse lines.

January 28th. Usual reconnoitring. Some rain, fine afternoon. Visited troop at Qurna, tea with Norfolks.

January 29th. In lines, shot two dogs, busy all day.

January 30th. Very heavy sniping by the enemy, got close to the perimeter, sounded just by our tents, killed ten, wounded and captured five. Reconnoitring saw groups returning from sniping, caught two, and charged a party of eight. Ground very bad, all water and nullahs, had to wade two nullahs, the enemy stood, we killed the lot. One man missed me four times, and then fortunately clubbed his rifle: I revolvered him, and then sabred another, sword went through like butter, all this time under heavy fire from ten to twelve, tried to reach them, but too much water, and had to take cover in stream. Dafadar Shiu Chand killed two yards away (after first charge). 'Amethyst' hit in neck, so had to change (horses). Under cover from fire of party, who had already returned, we retired; my horse immediately shot, and fell dead after going one hundred yards. Dafadar Mansa Ram returned and gave me his horse. Jemadar Ghasi Ram killed at first charge. Casualties, two men killed, three wounded, five horses killed, and five wounded.

January 31st. Very stiff. Busy, mail arrived yesterday, good letters. An attack expected to-night.

February 1st. Usual reconnoitring, nil.

February 2nd. In lines, busy building traverses.

Extract from ninth letter, dated 2-2-1915:—

"Tried to catch the Arabs out by putting flags attached some gun cotton which was bound to go off when the flag is pulled up; in each case the flag was taken, and a large hole made, but no remnants or blood about. The Viceroy comes here on Monday. I fancy his coming has large political significance, and means we are come to stay, and will doubtless have good effect amongst the Arabs. I have kept notes for future reference, in fact, my diary is fairly complete of all incidents we have been in. 'Amethyst,' I think will recover, she is much better to-day; they are sending all wounded horses to Basra. It would be so much simpler to bring the hospital up here, one would think, still, they get no sniping there, which is something. The General expects an attack to-night, so everything is ready. My bed is now on a level with the ground, and if heavy fire, I can roll off, so be two feet lower; also sand bags and earth works outside, so fairly safe. Every one has fortifications of sorts. Am building them in the squadron for the horses, but they take time as must be high and numerous to be of use: if only one could teach horses to lie down at a given signal! The camel shot was the only one standing up, the remainder have now front legs tied up, so that they cannot stand at night. Good news the 'Blucher' being sunk. I think we evidently had news of their coming."

[The following was an enclosure to the above letter, and is a detailed account of the affair which took place on January 30th and has already been mentioned in the diary for that date. I accordingly insert it below.]

"On the 30th of January we were out at 8-15 with three troops (sixty men) to cover a small force proceeding North up the left bank of the Tigris to burn a village; during the early hours of the morning, the camp had been very heavily fired on, four of our horses and one camel were killed, badly wounded several (five). The enemy had got quite close in, ten dead Turks were found, and five wounded ones in the morning. The enemy's fire was very heavy, and we expected the camp to be rushed, they were so close, but our maxims did good work. When we had proceeded about four miles, we saw several parties of the enemy retiring, evidently some of those who had attacked our camp. With two troops I tried to cut them off (while one troop covered the infantry, who were about three miles behind); we soon captured two, who when they saw it was useless, came towards us without firing. I had sent another section (six men) to capture them and escort them to camp. Proceeding soon came near several groups (of the enemy), one of eight being nearest, who began to open fire. I decided to charge them, when about two hundred yards away the going became very marshy, and we had to wade streams three or four feet deep, which of course we had to walk through, all the time under rapid fire of the eight close by, and about twelve, four hundred yards further off, and about another eight scattered about. (Their mausers make a horrid sharp crack-like sound.) Owing to the very marshy and broken ground, the pace was unfortunately slow. We closed and it was soon over; but all the time the rest of the enemy kept up a rapid fire. One of the eight men fired at me deliberately four times, and then lost his head, and clubbed his rifle, so I drew my revolver, putting my sword in my left hand. I had been shooting dogs the day before, and forgot to refill my revolver, two chambers empty, the third effort I missed, the fourth the poor wretch sat down violently. I then pursued a Turk, who was escaping, and a sowar and myself ran him through at the same time; it is wonderful how easily a sword goes in. My favourite, 'Amethyst,' was then badly hit in the neck, and I had to dismount (she covered me with blood) and get another horse, sending her back. The rest of the enemy were keeping up a most unpleasant fire, especially the twelve, so determined to go for them, had to cross a wider stream to get at them: having done so, the marsh became deeper, so when about three hundred yards off, thinking we should not be able to reach them, as several men had had falls and horses shot, I turned off, and took cover in the stream and replied to their fire. I held four horses while the men fired; in the meantime several of the dismounted men had opened fire further back, and my squadron officer having come up,—I had sent him on a message—directed rapid fire on the enemy, which relieved us of some of their attention, so I decided to get away out of a very unpleasant situation, standing waist deep in water under heavy fire. A dafadar was shot dead three yards from me, when retiring. I had only gone two hundred yards and crossed one stream when my horse was shot in the neck, and rolled over dead fifty yards further on. I was now almost the last; a dafadar seeing me running like a red shank, came back and gave his horse. (I have recommended him and hope he will get something) Having crossed the last stream, and soon collected all, and sent the wounded (three) men and horses away, retired. A most valuable Indian Officer had also been killed—the man he charged killed him dead at a few yards distance. My trumpeter had a very narrow escape. The man he was charging dropped his rifle suddenly as the trumpeter got quite close; this so startled his horse that it stopped dead. The Turk seeing the opportunity, seized his rifle again and fired, killing the horse dead (shot through the head,) the bullet coming out and hitting the trumpeter full in the chest, and knocking him endways, but making no wound, only a large bruise. The trumpeter had his own horse badly wounded during the previous night, so he was in for a bad run of luck. Five horses were killed and five wounded. I think we were very lucky in having so few men hit. It is not every day of one's life one assists in killing two of the enemy, and has two horses shot under one. The number of bullets that were flying about, one felt that an Almighty Providence was guarding one from being hit. I felt very thankful that night being safe and sound. After this skirmish went and covered the infantry operations. In the afternoon tried to recover the two bodies, but there were a number of Turks about who got in position, so gave it up, as useless having more casualties. There were several rumours in camp that I had been killed, also wounded; the latter arose from my being covered with blood from the two horses. Our wounded and men with disabled horses thought I had been hit for this reason. Then my own charger being led in gave rise to my being killed."

The following extract from a letter (received from a brother officer) found amongst my brother's correspondence reads as follows:—"I must congratulate you on the brilliant charge of your squadron the other day. I think it was a very fine performance, and it will buck up your people a lot, and give the Arabs a wholesome respect for you. I know these scattered groups of dismounted Arabs are awkward customers to tackle, I saw the squadrons at Elloui encountering some of them. I also congratulate on coming through untouched. I hope your old mare was not badly wounded and is recovered."

The following report was also amongst my brother's papers sent to me:—

"In continuation of my report B.M./33, dated 30th January 1915, on the action of the Mezera covering force on the left bank of the

Tigris on the 30th January 1915, I have the honour to bring to notice the gallant action of two troops of "A" squadron (about thirty sabres) of the 33rd Queen Victoria's Own Light Cavalry, led by Major M. H. Anderson of that regiment.

"2. Major Anderson came upon several groups of the enemy's riflemen, evidently the rear party of the enemy's force that had attacked our camp during the night. Two of the enemy were first captured. Major Anderson then proceeded to round up a group of eight hostile riflemen.

"3. The going was bad, marshy, and broken with nullahs, so the pace was slow. Two streams from three to four feet deep had to be crossed. The cavalry, however, closed.

"4. Throughout the charge they were under heavy rifle fire from this group, and from another group of twelve men some four hundred yards on their right flank. The group of eight men stood their ground, firing to the last. They were cut down to a man.

"5. Having despatched this group of eight, Major Anderson then advanced on the flank group of twelve. He found, however, the marsh and nullahs so increasingly difficult that he was obliged to abandon his enterprise against them. He took cover in a deep nullah, and finally withdrew under the support afforded by Captain Dickson, 29th Lancers (attached 33rd Cavalry) who came up at this juncture with several men he had collected who had lost their horses.

"6. In this action the casualties of the 33rd Cavalry were:—

Killed: 1 Jamadar, 1 Dafadar and 5 horses.

Wounded: 3 sowars and 5 horses.

The behaviour of all ranks was most satisfactory.

"7. I would particularly bring to notice the following as deserving of special recognition :—

"(1) Major M. H. Anderson, 33rd Queen Victoria's Own Light Cavalry.

"He led the charge against the enemy with conspicuous gallantry and resolution. He had two horses shot under him.

"(2) Captain H. E. Short, I.M.S.

'He attended the wounded in a most gallant and self-sacrificing manner, right up in the firing line under heavy rifle fire.

(3) Jemadar Ram Karan, 33rd Q.V.O. Light Cavalry, led his troop with dash, and was most collected in directing his men under trying conditions.

(4) Dafadar Mansa Ram, 33rd Q.V.O. Light Cavalry, during the hottest part of the action seeing that Major Anderson was dismounted (horse killed) returned under heavy fire and gave up his own mount to him."

In connection with the action of the 30th January 1915 at Mezera, in which my brother took part, the awards given to men of my brother's squadron ("A" Squadron) were:—

Admitted to the Second Class of the Indian Order of Merit (Military Division):

Jemadar Ram-Karan, 33rd Queen Victoria's Own Light Cavalry, for conspicuous conduct at Mezera on 30th January 1915. During the retirement of the enemy's forces he led his troop with commendable dash over marshy ground and under heavy rifle fire from front and flank, against several groups of the enemy's riflemen, and directed his men with much skill under trying circumstances.

Awarded the Indian Distinguished Service Medal:

No. 2292 Dafadar Mansaram, 33rd Q.V.O. Light Cavalry.

The following is an extract of the official despatches:—

The following despatch is gazetted from the General Officer Commanding Indian Expeditionary Force D., to the Chief of the General Staff, Army Headquarters, India, Simla:—

"As I am about to relinquish the command of the Indian Expeditionary Force D, I have the honour to submit for the favourable consideration of his Excellency the Commander-in-Chief the names of those officers and non-commissioned officers whose good services during the operations from November, 1914, to 31st March, 1915, I desire to bring to notice in addition to those who have already been mentioned in my reports No. 101 G. dated 7th December, and 174 G., dated 29th December, 1914.

"The following officers are specially brought to notice for gallantry in the field:—

"Major M. H. Anderson, 33rd Cavalry.—In the operation from Mezera on the left bank of the Tigris on 30th January, 1915, he led a successful charge against the enemy with conspicuous gallantry and resolution. He had two horses shot under him.

"Captain H. E. Short, I.M.S.—In the operations from Mezera on the left bank of the Tigris on 30th January, 1915, this medical officer displayed great devotion and courage in attending wounded in the open, in face of rifle fire at comparatively close quarters."

From what I have been able to gather about Dafadar Mansa Ram's gallantry I can only conclude that he saved my brother's life. A photograph of Dafadar Mansa Ram and other wounded soldiers appeared in the "Illustrated Times of India" dated June 2nd 1915, showing him wearing the Distinguished Service Medal, also the following paragraph, which I insert below.

D.S.M. FOR INDIAN SOLDIER.

"The accompanying photograph is of Dafadar Mansa Ram, of the Queen Victoria's Own Light Cavalry, who was presented with the D.S.M., at Saugor. He is with wounded soldiers from the Persian Gulf. Mansa Ram's squadron were retiring before a large body of the enemy and on looking round he noticed that his squadron commander, Major Anderson, had been left 300 yards behind and was being closely pressed by the enemy. Turning about he galloped back across three streams and with a 'point' here and a 'cut' there he disposed of the enemy who were surrounding Major Anderson. Major Anderson's horse was then shot through the head and Mansa Ram persuaded the Major to take his horse. Mansa Ram took a rifle and some cartridges. Creeping along the nullahs he met and disposed of more of the enemy and finally got back without a scratch. It was with deep grief that Mansa Ram heard that Major Anderson was subsequently killed in action on the 29th April."

It may be interesting to remark that Risaldar Dhokul Singh, 3rd Q.O. Bombay Light Cavalry (now 33rd Q.V.O. Light Cavalry), was advanced from the 2nd class to the 1st class of the Indian Order of Merit for conspicuous gallantry during the retreat from Maiwand on the 27th July 1880—(On which occasion he was instrumental in saving the life of (my father) Lieut.-Colonel H. S. Anderson,* 1st Bombay Native Infantry, who was severely wounded)—and in the attack on the village of Deh Kojah near Kandahar.

Diary continued.

February 3rd. Reconnoitring as usual, saw fine pig on way back.

February 4th. In lines, busy, thunderstorm about 9 p.m.

° Afterwards General Sir H. S. Anderson, K.C.B.

February 5th. Reconnoitring, saw nothing particular, Arabs fired at us about two miles. Went on H.M.S. "Miner," good view from top. Rode "Attala," first time for two weeks, very fat but not lame. About seven hundred Arabs on right bank with many flags, to bait us, a deal of waste of ammunition, as no observers. "Miner" firing a lot at sundown, must have hit some. Much fresher.

February 6th. In lines. Viceroy arrived and inspected the fortifications, saw him in the distance. Cold wind.

February 7th. Outposts, very cold wind. Viceroy left at 11-45. I went out in afternoon again.

February 8th. Dickson, chill kept quiet. Lines, building walls. Cold wind. Sniping at night, No. 5 Redoubt 119th, killed one and wounded several, blood tracks.

February 9th. Reconnoitring, heard Arabs chanting quite three miles off, must have been considerable body of them, saw a few flags. Much warmer. Went out again at 3-30.

Extract from tenth letter dated 9-2-1915:—"Have had three days of biting N. wind, but now has gone South, and is raining, so hope to-morrow will be fine; rain is beastly, as at night keeps one awake in a tent. Have nothing particular to recount, here outposts every other day, and building walls to protect the horses the other. A wire to-night saying at Shaiba we had one man killed and two wounded, but no details of how or when it occurred. One sniper was killed last night, and several from blood tracks were wounded, but could not be found this morning, expect got away in a boat. Reinforcements have arrived, but suppose better not say how many. All the wounded horses have been sent to Basra, including 'Amethyst,' who is getting on well, but bullet still in; one would have thought it much easier to have brought the Veterinary Hospital, or part of it up here. Many thanks for the papers, they come regularly. Very glad the Turks have taken the knock in Egypt, wish it had been worse. I think I was exceedingly fortunate on the 30th, and feel the Almighty was guiding me all the time, as must have been under a sharp fire for some fifteen minutes at least. My 'lungi' having fallen off of course made me more conspicuous within short range; when I wear another shall have it tied on."

Diary continued.

February 10th. In lines. Detachment 22nd Cavalry, twenty-two horses and twenty-six Sikhs arrived. Colder.

February 11th. Very cold, reconnoitring as usual.

February 12th. In lines. A (1) came over from Qurna. Cold wind. Rode to Brick Kilns, three pig came right up to the redoubt, one swam the Shwab River.

February 13th. Very cold wind. Reconnoitring, floods increasing, two to three hundred pig out, ten killed, fine boars, watching a good run as H.M.S. "Miner" fired at sand dunes, quite good shot. Very cold outside camp. A little sniping about 9 into Camp Tigris. Our searchlights working both sides of the river.

February 14th. In camp.

February 15th. Reconnoitring as usual; cold wind.

February 16th. Some rain at night, cold wind. South gale most unpleasant. Little sniping.

Extract from eleventh letter dated Mezerah, 16-2-1915:—

"Nothing particular to tell you. The floods are increasing enormously, and how long we shall be able to be here is a problem. Hundreds of pig have been driven out of the marshes, and a good many speared, but spears are very scarce indeed. I hope to get two from the Ordnance but have not come as yet, so have only been a spectator, as with a sword it is too risky, one would be sure to get one's horse cut, as these pig are full of fight; going to the outposts yesterday put up one quite close, a great fluffy creature. The Arabs, several hundreds of them, came to within five thousand yards of camp the other day with about one hundred standards. They do it on purpose for us to shell them, and don't seem to mind a bit, (but) enjoy the show. I went out with two guns, and then they were two thousand yards away, all sitting and standing round the flags, while shell came over them. When we opened (fire) with the two (guns) at two thousand yards they ran back, some taking the flags, and some leaving them, but returned directly we retired; really most extraordinary people, as they cannot reply, having no guns. Intelligence say that four German officers have just arrived at the enemy's camp. At Shaiba, Gillies had a bit of a show. He went with a squadron to reconnoitre Ajaimi's Camp, about eighteen miles away, did so, and was followed home for fifteen miles by two hundred Arab horsemen and sixty Turkish; had one man and two horses killed, two men and seven horses wounded; quite exciting. The Sikh's body was brought in by three men, the Arabs were within two hundred yards, firing at them when they rescued it. A very plucky performance, but I don't think unnecessary risks should be taken. Of course one likes to bury one's dead. Tremendous gale from the South to-day, very unpleasant, and a good deal of rain last night, so the usual mud this morning. We are rather tired of this place, and should like a change, especially as the country is being curtailed so. The following awards were notified and granted to the three men for their gallantry in recovering the Sikh's body.

"Granted the Indian Order of Merit, Second Class:

"No. 2571 Lance-Dufadar Arjun Singh, 33rd Queen Victoria's Own Light Cavalry, for conspicuous gallantry at Shaiba on 9th February 1915, when during a reconnaissance, he, assisted by Sowars No. 3089 Buta Singh and No. 3357 Mangal Singh, succeeded under the close fire of the enemy in hoisting on to the front of his saddle the dead body of a comrade and bringing it back to the main body of the reconnoitring party, and subsequently conveying it to Shaiba Post.

"Awarded the Indian Distinguished Service Medal:

"33rd Queen Victoria's Own Light Cavalry. No. 3089 Sowar Buta Singh. No. 3357 Sowar Mangal Singh."

Diary continued.

February 17th. Reconnoitring, Arabs came out of sand dunes and fired at us, coming back followed for some considerable distance. Warmer. Floods very high by river and land. Gunner road in great danger, much work going on.

February 18th. Much warmer. Grantham, Dickson and self out pig sticking at two, Dickson got one good boar (33",) and after a great run Grantham and self killed a boar (30"). Enjoyable afternoon. Complimentary remarks by Sir A. Barrett on skirmish of 30th communicated to me. Sheepshanks with 30 or 40 with Hydrat Ali proceeded with flying column to Nasiri last Sunday.

February 19th. Reconnoitring, saw no end of pig, two dogs cut out and nearly did for a squeaker. Dickson shot dogs, hawk attacking fox, but our arrival ended struggle. L. D. Ram Singh missing, hope he is alright, suppose he is afraid to approach the searchlights and redoubts.

February 20th. (In) lines. Rained all last night. Ram Singh turned up in the morning none the worse, the searchlight directed him, but feared to be shot if approached redoubt. The whole place a quagmire. Mail letters.

Extract from twelfth letter dated Saturday, 20th Feb. 1915 :—

"We are slowly being flooded out of this. The water is rising by leaps and bounds, and there is now a considerable stretch (only shallow of course) between the Turks and ourselves, so expect we shall be moved in a few days South, and I had better not say where for fear of the Censor. The reinforcements reached here all alright. I expect they did not want another expedition but made all preparations, just to show that one could be sent if necessary. We expect to hear of fighting West of Basra against a Chief called Ajaimi with a large following, and I hope they round him up properly. There has been a scrap near Ahwaz, and some of our men are casualties, Sheepshanks is there with a few. I could give you details of force but better abstain Went out after pig on 'Attala,' with Grantham and Dickson and got two. 'Attala' did not like the first one, but went quite well after the second; intended going to-day, but too wet. The Arab sniping party three nights ago left the officer behind them shot in the knee. They had not been for some days close up, only a few shots fired a long way off, a few casualties keep them from being too bold. Your long letter of the 7th arrived to-day. Many thanks for the nibs, also the magazine and papers. I am very lucky in that all my letters have reached unmutilated. Grantham wrote a long one home, and nearly everything cut out; it seems so senseless, as it has all appeared in the papers what we have done, and where."

(This letter was opened by the Censor.)

Diary continued.

February 21st. Lovely day, floods increasing enormously. To Qurna with Onslow, the country to the West, water to the horizon.

February 22nd Went out with Grantham after pig, no luck, very few, and all deep in water, got bogged twice, and then gave it up.

February 23rd. Patrolling, water increasing rapidly, took spears but saw nil approachable. Mountain battery very lucky, got three pig right in the open with no trouble. The Arabs (about fifty) came down much further than usual, so fired a few volleys, which sent them back.

February 24th. Head Quarters and two troops left for Basra. Dickson, self and two others after pig, roused one very angry boar, could have escaped but refused, hardly any run, but charged all. I got the spear, wrenched my wrist, no run, but very massive tushes. (boar 32½). Afternoon watched two boar killed by Mountain battery, one long run.

February 25th. Embarked Blosh Lynch, began 9 a.m. Very warm, very pretty towards sundown. Got all mules and kit off by 8 p.m. Slept on board.

February 26th. Completed disembarking, got to lines with all kit 9-30, began soon after 6. Fresh morning, lovely day. On river in evening with Willoughby, who was not feeling very fit.

February 27th. Busy all day, went to Ordnance Depôt, Base Depôt, and Pay Office. Farrier Changi Lal died, galloping consumption.

February 28th. Started at 8-45, reached Shaiba 3-30. Very hot, water a foot deep more than half the way, very dusty camp, poisonous place. Felt the sun in a "lungi," so changed.

March 1st. With two squadrons, two guns R.H.A. to South Mound, Look-out Tower and towards Ratifia, hot and dull. Watered at 1 p.m. near Zoubair.

March 2nd. Moved camp, much better place. High winds all day with dust. Headache and feverish. Sixty of my squadron on night duty. March 3rd. Started at 6-30. (Four guns R.H.A., three squadrons 33rd, three squadrons 16th), reconnaissance. Stack in command, advance regiment saw two hundred (enemy) on the way out, went ten miles towards their camp. Guns shelled, but were very short, began to retire 1-45, and enemy's horsemen to advance, by successive retirements of squadrons reached Shwebda all right, and from there they (the enemy) seemed to fall back, but suddenly being reinforced pressed the retreat, during which dear Grantham and Willoughby were killed. Santa saved Willoughby once.

Casualties on 3rd at	B.O.s killed	B.O.s wounded	I.O.s killed	I.O.s wounded	Men killed	Men wounded
SHAIBA	2	1	1	-	3	8
AHWAZ	-	1	-	1	5	5

	Horses killed	Horses wounded	Men missing
SHAIBA	2	18	1
AHWAZ	7	2	2

March 4th. Very busy. Funeral of five British Officers, including Willoughby and Grantham. The O.C. read part of the service. Bad cold and headache. Hear enemy lost five Sheikhs yesterday.

March 5th. Our day out. Self and Meiklejohn saw several hundred of the enemy's cavalry, but only (a) few came close. Force turned out on my report. Felt very seedy so went to bed early, had severe pains about 3-30, so had to call doctor in who gave some medicine, felt better a few hours later. Alarm in evening, all stood to places.

March 6th. Head much better, but kept to tent, better towards evening.

Extract from thirteenth letter dated Shaiba, 6-3-1915:—"A sad, sad letter. As you will already have seen in the papers, Willoughby and Grantham were killed yesterday, and Colonel Stack wounded. We (six squadrons, 16th and ourselves, and four guns R.H.A.) went out to create a diversion while guns on ships shelled their camp. Of course nothing happened on the way out, and only a few of the enemy seen, but directly the retirement commenced, their horsemen followed, and as is their wont, always try to work round your flanks; all went well for the first six miles, for the first three of which we (the 33rd) retired by successive squadrons, covering each other's retirement by fire action; they then began to threaten the flanks, so the 16th came in, also the guns, but the going was very bad for the guns, and they delayed us a good deal as their horses got done; after going about six miles, we thought the enemy had had enough, and we seemed to be leaving them; when they received reinforcements, and became bolder, coming on and firing at only two and three hundred yards. They fire mounted, so do little damage unless they get quite close. The enemy were now somewhat unpleasantly near, and Colonel Stack charged the enemy, and did considerable damage to them, he had his left thumb shot away by the same shot, I fancy, that wounded him in the body, also a sword cut on his right hand. Grantham was shot in the back and head, and Willoughby during the charge, I think. We had six killed and nine wounded, sixteen horses wounded and several killed. This is a poisonous hole, blows with fury every other day, and the air is full of dust, the water tastes like Epsom's Salts, and I have not felt well since I arrived, have a severe cold and no voice. We are now cut off from Busra by six miles of water, one to three feet deep, and everything has to come through the water on mules—killing work. Sir A. B. officially wrote he had hoped to personally congratulate me (on my little show), but suddenly returning to Basra had prevented him."

In the official despatch (the same one in which my brother and Captain Short, I.M.S., were mentioned for gallantry in the field) Colonel Stack and Lieut. Sheepshanks, 12th Cavalry (attached 33rd

L.C.) were also mentioned for gallantry in the field, and I think this is a very opportune place to insert the extract here as the affair has just been described above. "Lieutenant-Colonel C. S. Stack, 33rd Cavalry.—Severely wounded near Shaiba on 3rd March, 1915, whilst displaying great personal gallantry and handling his regiment in a most skilful manner. This officer did extremely good work whilst commanding the Shaiba post for over two months.

"Lieutenant R. H. Sheepshanks, 12th Cavalry (attached 33rd Cavalry), was conspicuous for his gallantry and skilful handling on March, 1915. Reforming his troop he repeatedly charged the foremost lines of the enemy and inflicted heavy loss on them."

The following admissions to the Military Division of the Indian Order of Merit (2nd class) were also notified.

Risaldar Santa Singh, 33rd Queen Victoria's Own Light Cavalry; No. 2492 Dafadar Bishan Singh, 33rd Queen Victoria's Own Light Cavalry; No. 2829 Sowar Buda Singh, 33rd Queen Victoria's Own Light Cavalry, for conspicuous bravery and devotion to duty near Shaiba on the 3rd March, 1915, in charging through a body of Arab horsemen to the assistance of Captain Willoughby (killed in action) who was surrounded on all sides.

March 7th. Feeling seedy, out to support Meiklejohn, but the enemy did not come on.

March 8th. 16th out, enemy advanced in numbers, and some firing, everything ready (for an attack), all tents down, very uncomfortable night, but not very cold.

March 9th. Onslow fever. Our day out, no alarms, much warmer at night.

March 10th. Our day in, quiet. Managed to water ninety of our horses at fresh well, just dug, and how the poor wretches drank. General Kennedy for our brigade arrived. Lieut. LeMesurier, I.A.R., joined us. News three German submarines sunk by merchantmen.

March 11th. We, two battalions, and four guns R.H.A. to Barjisiyeh Wood cover cutting wood, and to destroy Arab encampment if found; not found. Force began to retire about 1-30, our advanced scouts fired on at long range. My squadron protective cavalry till 5-30, in by 6, then watered. Watered in B. Wood at 2-30, horses had two good drinks.

March 12th. Our day in, all quiet and no scares, rifle and sword inspection. Sold Grantham's and Ferris' horses Rs. 1,000 each; much warmer. [I presume for "Ferris," Willoughby should be read. E.A.]

March 13th. Very windy and dusty, in lines all day busy.

March 14th. Dickson left for Ahwaz. Busy.

Extract from fourteenth letter dated Shaiba, Sunday, 14-3-15:—

"Have had a nice quiet day, and no wind, which is a great blessing, as yesterday was awful, and everything is impregnated with dust. We sadly miss Willoughby and Grantham; the former was very fond of art, painting, etc., on which he wrote good articles, was exceedingly very clever in his way; he was also one of the most sweet-tempered beings in the world, full of fun, and always bright and amusing. He was very fond of me, and I of him. Grantham I was exceedingly fond of too, a sterling comrade, most hardworking and conscientious, and whatever he undertook to do was most thoroughly done. Stack is going on well, should like to go in and see him, but as half the road between here and Basra is water, have to sleep the night in Basra, as have to go with the convoy. Small boats have been able to come out, and some of the convoy work is being done by them, which relieves pressure. The 16th Lancers had a bad day in France—six officers killed and six wounded by a mined trench. The war is really terrible, one longs to go on active service, but when it is terrible like in Europe, and one's own officers are killed, one begins to think there has been enough. The horses would not drink the brackish water here to start with, and fell off much in condition, but nearly all are drinking it now. There is nearly a fresh well from which the fastidious ones are watered: when they won't drink, they won't eat. 'Amethyst' is in Basra, but came out here. Of course she disliked the water, and consequently did not improve, so sent her back, and hope she will pick up. When she arrived she was looking thin. We are horribly short of officers: an I.A.R. Officer has just joined us. One wonders how long we shall be here, all sorts of rumours are about, but I don't believe any one knows at all what is going to be done. Sheepshanks has I think broken two ribs in a show at Ahwaz. 17th. Had a bit of a fight yesterday. The enemy came as if to attack our camp, and we retired fighting before them, drawing them on; unfortunately they stopped when about two thousand yards away. Whether our R.A. was too much for them, don't know, but we all hoped they really were going to push up against our infantry, but no such luck. P.S. We live in strenuous times, always ready, and seldom take our clothes off; am getting accustomed to sleeping in boots. We had no tents last night, and it rained about half an inch, and found I was in a pool this morning, my canvas bed had collected it all,—somewhat damp."

Diary continued.

March 15th. Our turn, my squadron out 12 to 6-30, got in and watered just before 7; saw no one.

March 16th. Enemy attacked. Their horsemen (came) round West side of the camp, they killed four of the 16th, and wounded four of the squadron just gone out. Brigade out at 8, and retired slowly before their infantry. Massy with "D" got into action against their infantry in close order at twelve hundred yards. R.H.A. fired well, our R.F.A. enfiladed them nicely, when within two thousand yards of our position they retired. Back in camp about 2-30. Every one still in complete readiness on posts, no tents, rained most of the night.

March 17th. Three British Officers patrols out at 6-30, my squadron (out) at 8, saw nil, relieved by Meiklejohn at 1-30.

March 18th. Infantry out cutting wood, our brigade went out to round up sheep if found between wood and Shwebda; there were some, but on the far side, so did not bring them in, watered at Shwebda, and retired, saw twelve horsemen. In camp before 1, had a sleep, dined with the R.H.A. Quiet night, mail in.

March 19th. Quiet day.

March 20th. Brigade parade practising retirements, always a difficult problem; but hope shall be soon advancing.

March 21st. Brigade parade, thought retirements much too long, don't like it done at the gallop.

Extract from fifteenth letter dated Shaiba, 21-3-1915:—

"No letters from you, but your papers, for which many thanks. The enemy advanced on the 16th, cavalry and infantry, about three thousand of them. Their horsemen unfortunately killed four and wounded four of the 16th, one squadron of which was out early as protective cavalry. We (our brigade) went out and fought a retiring action, and inflicted some loss, one of our squadrons getting them in close formation at twelve hundred yards, and the guns too; they retired when about one and half miles from our position—unfortunate, as the infantry would have given a good account of themselves;

us in trenches and they in the open would have been a pleasant change. Our Brigade fired at least thirteen thousand (rounds) besides R.H.A. My trumpeter's horse was hit through the stomach, lucky not mine, as he was holding her too. One other of ours was wounded and that was all. All sorts of rumours are about as to what and where we are going, but I won't mention them."

Diary continued.

March 22nd. Nothing doing, quiet day.

March 23rd. 7th and 16th started at 1 a.m. to round up sheep South of Barjiseyeh Wood, one of our squadrons and R.H.A. following at dawn. Five hundred sheep, eleven friendly Arabs, and some women (two wounded by bullets) brought in, and several of the enemy killed; the 16th three men and five horses wounded.

March 24th. Much hotter.

March 25th. Quiet day. Put out standing patrols.

March 26th. Protection duty, after rain very clear, cloudy, and very little mirage.

March 27th. South wind blowing dust.

March 28th. Started 2 a.m., back 10-30. Marched to South-east end wood, then a "chukker" round, saw a few enemy, but personally think sheep guards. Sheep some way out, did nil. Awful wind and dust.

Extract from sixteenth letter dated Shaiba, 28-3-1915:—

"This is the most poisonous day we have had, blowing a hurricane and the whole place dust and sand: one eats, breathes, and swallows little else. This morning we started out at 2 a.m., marched till 4-45, and then waited till 5-30, the idea being to round up any sheep or enemy found. We found some sheep, though a long way out, and it would have taken a long time driving them home, so we left them alone. About a week ago we rounded up five hundred sheep, and killed several of the enemy. There seems to be rumours that the war will soon end, but I can't see what reasons they have for thinking so; the Germans have done wonderfully—still in France, nearly all Belgium, and in Russia; we must get into German territory, even if peace is declared soon. Armies of the Allies should be quartered in and march throughout Germany; not that I think war is over by any means, but hope this year will see the end of it. I did not mean not to incur risk in recovering wounded, but I can't see the use of risking men's lives to recover the bodies of men known to be dead. Dickson writes from Ahwaz, says it is a very good place, the fight was very severe. About sixty of the Dorsets did wonders: some of their N.C.O's. took command of double companies of the 7th Rajputs, when their officers were killed, and handled them in fine style. I think it is a mistake appointing I.A.R. officers, they naturally know nil, and one has not time to teach them. In six months they will of course pick up a good deal; till then it means the rest of us have all the more to do. Now if they had given us some British N.C.O's. with any temporary rank they liked, they would have been useful, from British cavalry, who could easily have sent say two or three to a regiment. It is the stiffening qualities of men who know their business that one wants—these are the sort to give confidence to troops. Your gift to the squadron has arrived—they were very pleased—I duly distributed them. The Indian Officer who was with me in my skirmish has got the Indian Order of Merit, and the Dafadar who brought back his horse to me the Distinguished Service Medal, so I am quite pleased; also two of the latter, and one Indian Order of Merit to men of our Sikh squadron, for going back and bringing in a corpse under very heavy fire. Very plucky, of course, one likes to always do it, but is the risk justifiable? I think not."

Diary continued.

March 29th. Quiet day, did mess accounts.

March 30th. Brigade parade, Zoubair way, wind in North, much pleasanter.

March 31st. About ten shots fired into camp from North, alarm went and we stood to arms, and on posts, till midnight. Bright moon; two squadrons 7th ordered out and infantry, but saw nil.

April 1st. Out at 8 to support South Mound Patrol, saw two horsemen and about fifty infantry, who retired about three miles from fort. Onslow relieved me midday. Feeling very seedy, so to bed, fever.

April 2nd. Feeling very seedy, fever and chill, in bed all day, mail arrived, good letters.

April 3rd. No fever this morning, but not feeling up to much, milk diet very uninteresting.

April 4th. Better, got up.

Extract from seventeenth letter, dated Shaiba, Easter Sunday, 4-4-15:—"I have been laid up for the last three days with, as Pepys would say, fever and a naughty colic and griping of the vital organs—I think a chill. About ten shots were fired at camp at long range, so the alarm went, and we all (were) at our posts till midnight (*i.e.*, three hours): the infantry went out and two squadrons at 11 p.m. (it was moonlight) but found nothing. As it was not particularly cold I did not put on a coat till I felt it chilly, when presume the mischief was done. Was out the next day feeling seedy, and on returning 1 p.m. found had fever and went to bed. The weather here is really wonderful; forty lbs. tents are not the coolest of things, but not unpleasant so far, and to-day the air is quite cool. This new rule is a great gain being able to promote N.C.Os. in place of those wounded or sick, all carrying pay, and becoming permanent after a month will help much to efficiency I think."

April 5th. Got up (at) 9, did a good deal of interior economy work. The Brigadier insisted on my going over to his room, did so after breakfast, delightful after a 40lbs. tent, the General kindness itself, slept well but woke early.

April 6th. Head much better, but still have a good deal of pain; in fort all day. G.O.C. most kind. 18th Brigade arrived (three regiments).

April 7th. Brigadier absolutely forbid me to return to lines, awful day, hurricane from South, and dust terrible till evening, worst day we have had. Regiment shifting camp, visited squadron in evening.

April 8th. Lovely day, bright sun. Brigadier would not let me out. Ricketts calls me "The Prisoner of Shaiba." Intelligence reports German Staff Officers with Turks having eighteen regular battalions and some quick-firers, bribed all the Kurds to return, and are going to attack in force shortly.

April 9th. Wind South-east, so lots of flies. Brigade parade, I on foot to see if two squadrons moving from water can be seen from top of fort all the way to North Mound.

April 10th. G.O.C. allowed me to return to the regiment, feeling ever so much better.

April 11th. Brigade parade to dig trenches only half mile off to support protective troops; some thousands marching to Shwebda and Barjasiyeh, relieved by 7th at 12. Out again, whole brigade at 4, G.O.C. ordered me to fort, enemy only trying to reconnoitre. We had only one wounded, my trumpeter, not dangerous.

April 12th. Enemy's rifle fire began 5-10, and guns 5-30 a.m. Brigade just started towards Zoubair, but recalled. Camp heavily shelled for an hour, and then intermittently all day. Rifle fire heavy for ten minutes, just before dinner (bullets) came whistling over our tents. Mess tent unbearable most of the day. Heavy rifle fire at night, intermittently till morning, after which slept well. Our mess tents seemed special mark for enemy's shells.

April 13th. Mounted attack on North Mound, 7th leading. Brigadier thought opposition too great and retired. 7th had eighteen horses killed, and thirty-seven wounded. Major Wheeler killed. Brigade out at 2 with 16th Brigade, brought in two field guns. We charged Turkish regiment, who would all have thrown down their arms, but retreat sounded. We quite cleared out right flank. 16th Brigade took South Mound after half an hour R.A. preparation. 104th lost fifty, two British Officers killed.

April 14th. Division started out at 7 a.m. to take South Mound Ridge, Cavalry Brigade to watch right flank. When we reached due West of South Mound about fifteen hundred yards came under cross fire from there and North of wood; our R.H.A. soon silenced rifle firing from South Mound, knocking over several horsemen. About six squadrons sent to one thousand yards West of Look-Out Tower, and remained there till relieved by infantry, fairly continuously in action. Large bodies of enemy's infantry moving South-west toward Shwebda. We moved further West and were shelled, "B" squadron losing several horses. Then made flank attack on foot on trenches North-west of wood to relieve pressure on infantry in which were successful, but about 5, four squadrons and two guns ordered to left flank division, (being) supposed (to be) threatened by cavalry, but saw nil; reached camp 7-30, dark.

April 15th. Out three squadrons under Major Mears, 16th, as advance guard to force, collecting our dead and bringing in wounded Turks. Found their camp intact at Barjasiyeh—tents, kit, hospital, and large stores of ammunition (rifle and gun) three hundred boxes of shells. We had no chance of loot as had to guard South flank. Started back 6-20, reached camp about 7-30. Evidently given enemy great blow, all cleared off. Wounded Turks very grateful, about six hundred prisoners unwounded.

April 16th. Day in camp. Massy with three troops (part of force) covering removing of enemy's munitions. Dust storm in evening. Orders to move to Basra to-morrow received at 8 p.m.

April 17th. Started at 8-15. I rear guard to 63rd (battery) R.F.A. One gun and three waggons bogged before reaching water, had to drag out by hand, and took about one hour. Water practically the whole six miles except few islands (four very small ones). Gave two men of the Dorsets (a) lift on spare horses. Some misunderstanding on arrival as to where we should camp.

April 18th. Very stuffy. Went to Ordnance and S. & T. with Massy in "ballum" (a kind of boat), most restful; the green delightful after so much dust. Visited Hopwood at Head Quarters. Thunderstorm for half an hour at 4-15. Distributing kit.

April 19th. With Massy after breakfast to get Ordnance and S. & T. kit, back at 1, with former only, as "ballum" full. Sir J. Nixon came about 4-30, and was very complimentary. Busy distributing kit. Cool night, slept out in open.

April 20th. Exercise, after stables went to D.D.O. and Stationary Depôt, back to lunch. Wrote letters. Visited men in hospital, and Onslow. River very high. Clouded over and some rain at 9-30.

April 21st. Rained in evening. Visited "Amethyst" and decided to have her shot as looking terribly thin, sores, and breathing permanently wrong. Squadron fitted out fairly well with Ordnance stores and new breeches—a great thing.

[The eighteenth and nineteenth letters I received came together. The first is dated "Shaiba, 14th April 15," and is an account of the action which took place on the 13th and 14th. It is of course written from a cavalry point of view.]

Extract from eighteenth letter :—

"Am commencing this during an action which commenced this morning at 5-10 a.m. and it is now 10-5 a.m. The enemy yesterday advanced from their camp 18 miles off to some wells called Shwebda about 8 miles from here, and some to a wood three miles nearer, and last evening attempted to reconnoitre, but our Brigade went out and prevented it, but I fancy they must know a good deal from spies. We were told to expect an attack after midnight, but their infantry did not come till dawn and commenced firing at some very long range at 5-10, and their artillery about 5-30, shortly before ours did. They were rather short to start with, but soon settled down and for about an hour shells were screaming all over the place—most unpleasant. As our guns got their position, their fire slackened, but they start again about every 15 or 20 minutes; fortunately a lot of their shells don't burst till they strike the ground, one has just fallen about a hundred yards away. Our infantry have fired very little so far but a certain amount of maxim fire, they are reserving it till the enemy get close. I believe they are only about a thousand yards away, lying and scraping holes, very unlike their usual tactics, but they have some Germans with them. They have been threatening our flanks, but retired under shell fire. We are I think in a very strong position: our east is entirely protected by floods and our flanks rest on the water, our defences being in a semicircle. (Three more shells just arrived in vicinity). What the enemy intends to do I wonder. (1) Are they going to try and creep nearer and then about sundown make a rush ? (2) Will they get fed up during the day and retire in two or three hours, as they have not tasted our rifle fire yet, and are some miles from water, and it is a hot day? Our time does not really commence till they retire, and presumably we press their retirement. One rather hopes they will come closer and have a taste of rifle fire from our concealed trenches; poor wretches, if we give them a good doing, it will probably finish the business here. We expect they are attacking at Awaz also to-day. Our guns fire intermittently the whole time, also maxims and dropping rifle fire.

"16th instant. Have had no time to write I since began so have missed the mail. Well, shelling continued all day on the 12th, and was most unpleasant at times, and our mess tent a place to avoid, shells bursting all round. When dark, rifle fire began, and when washing my hands for dinner had to lie in my tent while the bullets fairly whistled. I then scuttled to mess (which is a dug out), and we all dined on the floor with the minimum of light. Till midnight at intervals bullets came over thick. From 12th to 16th (both inclusive) we have had 78 horses killed and wounded out of 340. On the 13th we were told to parade at 8-45 and while going to water two shells burst right over head and rifle bullets fell fast. One officer in the battery was wounded. Our brigade was told to try and gallop an intrenched position about one mile away: if the leading regiment found it too strongly held we are to retire. We all started off (no artillery preparation was made) and bullets fell fast, our artillery did not commenced firing till we started. In a few minutes we were ordered back as it was considered too strongly held, the leading squadrons losing heavily. About 2 p.m. the infantry took this position with a good many casualties, about a hundred, but after the place had been vigourously shelled for quite half an hour, our Brigade and one infantry one moved out about 4 o'clock to finish the enemy's left flank and bring in two mountain guns the enemy had abandoned. Our artillery R.H.A. knocked over several of the enemy's horsemen by very pretty shooting, the rest flying. We soon came up with a battalion of Turks: about one hundred were killed and if we had only gone on for another half mile should have captured four or five hundred. Unfortunately we were ordered to retire just too soon, and several already captured had to be left, most regrettable. Anyhow the enemy's left flank was entirely broken. We had a peaceful night which was a great luxury. The next day the larger portion of the force started out at 8 (I forgot to say General Melliss came out on the night of the 19th and took command of the Division as Sir A. Barrett had gone back on sick leave) to attack the enemy's right, and if possible cut off his retreat which his left, having gone, left rather open. We guarded the right and having pushed on, were soon under a cross fire, but our guns soon cleared the enemy out on our left, which was held by infantry, as soon as they arrived. Masses of the enemy's infantry could be seen retreating towards Shwebda as we pushing along the South Mound ridge threatened their line of retreat. The cross fire above referred to came from South Mound as we were about two thousand yards North of Beriisiyah Wood, and about 1,200 yards W.S.W. of South Mound. Five squadrons of the Brigade were pushed on as soon as our infantry reached South Mound to a ridge 1,200 yards W. of Watch Tower and were heavily engaged, several thousands of the enemy retiring towards the wood. When the infantry came up our Brigade Wess so as to still more threaten the enemy's flank, and several shells burst right amongst our horses, so we retired. Our Brigade just previous to these shells arriving contemplated a charge on the retiring foe, but fortunately did not try as there were several thousand infantry beside six guns at Shwebda and two or four on W. edge of wood. Our infantry at this time got stuck up by lines of enemy's trenches. To relieve the pressure we made a dismounted attack on their flank, which we hear had the desired effect, the enemy commenced to go and relaxed the fire on our infantry. During this time bullets were flying all about and we all must have had many narrow escapes. Collins had one through his helmet. About five we and one squadron (7th) were ordered to go and protect the retirement of Division on the left as it was supposed to be threatened by cavalry, but we saw none. It was unfortunate our being sent away, as we were doing useful work. I believe our casualties during the day were about 1,100 but expect you already know more than we do. The Dorsets had 17 (out of 24) officers casualties, including 4 killed, and 178 men, Norfolks about the same number in men; the other regiments had all 100 (about). The result is really a great victory: two mountain guns and three machine guns captured, at least six hundred prisoners (Turks) not counting about 150 wounded prisoners, all their camp tents, equipment, three hundred boxes of shells, 25 drums of powder, and boxes of small arms ammunition. They evidently left in a great hurry, and we presume all their transport was required to remove wounded, as prisoners say hundreds were sent back and they had not enough for munitions, etc. I don't know what they lost in killed, but on the 12th, 13th and 14th must have been not far short of thousand; a hundred and twenty-seven were counted in one trench. I was out on the 14th, day after the battle, but there was no sign of the enemy, we were out to examine their camp and bringing in our dead, and wounded Turks. Poor wretches, they were most grateful and kissed our hands, of course in many cases they were dying of thirst (I don't mean it literally). We did not get back to camp till nearly 8 yesterday and the day before. To-day has been our first rest for several days. Just got orders that we are to march bag and baggage to-morrow to Basra. Where we are destined for no one knows or why this sudden move.

"Sunday 18th. Basra. Our losses on 12th, 13th, 14th were 18 Officers killed, 37 wounded, and total casualties 1,289, I think, of which about 250 killed. The result seems to have been splendid, the Turks all falling back to Nasira, about 100 miles off. We had a horrid march in, I was rear guard to the battery, and one gun and 2 wagons got bogged, and it took us an hour to pull them out by hand with about 60 men. We marched through water for 6 or 7 miles, most tiring to the horses and you can imagine what it is for infantry. I gave two of the Dorsets lifts on spare horses, they were with the Mule convoy and got left behind. We arrived eventually at our destination, there was, however, some uncertainty as to where we should camp, so it took us some little time to reach our camping ground; this was certainly a little annoying, especially after a distinctly trying and tedious march. We, however, reached our camp after a short time, and very glad we were to get to it. The staff expressed their regret that there had been a little hitch over our camping arrangements. Our return to Basra seems to have been suddenly decided on, and our delay on the march, owing to the amount of water about, was also another factor to be contended with, so these two things may have been the cause of our not reaching our camp as soon as we had hoped.

Saw H————to-day, full of life; he is on Sir J. N.————Staff. Sir J. N. visited us yesterday and was very complimentary. The Turks are reported to have retreated and to be retiring miles, and have left at their second camp lots of gun ammunition, besides dead and wounded. So it seems to have been a real victory with far reaching results.

"All the prisoners were unanimous in saying our artillery fire was very accurate."

Extract from nineteenth letter dated Basra, 21-4-1915:—

"We are moving to-morrow, but can't say where. This last few days has been a pleasant change from dust. Heavy rain last night so now much cooler. This is, I should say, a far better climate than India. I went to see Onslow in hospital, he was shot on the 13th, in the shoulder, not bad, but bullet still in; a poor fellow paralyzed, bullet in the spine, dreadful, is it not? I did not hear what hope they had of him; another man I know five wounds; Colonel Clarkson, second-in-command, Dorsets, right elbow joint shattered, which the doctor told me is agony, he said it was a bad day with him. The hospital side of war is terrible. I had to sign 'Amethyst's' death warrant to-day and gave her a last feed of lucern. Her breathing is permanently injured, and one very hot day they thought would have to put a tube in, she was roaring so, and this standing still, also has become awfully thin, much worse than a month ago. Of course should like to put her in a green field, but that being impossible, think a bullet most merciful. The flies are dreadful, nearly drive one mad. No thanks, I don't want anything particular, unless you send me a small box of toothpicks, am reduced to grass. I missed last mail, I really could not attempt it, I ought to have posted on the 15th but did not return to camp till 8 p.m., having started at 7 a.m., and having had the three previous days it was too much, but you know no news means all well, only busy. Sir J. was round here, and very complimentary to us. Wish we had some more regular officers, dreadfully short."

Diary continued.

April 22nd. Rained early, and about 5 p.m. Camp very wet. Ordered to embark at 7 a.m. Began to load 11-30, all in camp by 8, great trouble in getting rations and kit over quagmire near camp.

April 23rd. In camp, waiting for mules to take our kit till 2-30, when started; soon clouded up and rain and thunder about 5-30, lightning very bright, we luckily escaped with little rain, but heavy (rain) all round. Reached camp Manduwan at 8; shared tent with C.O. March, seventeen miles.

April 24th. Started at 9-20 for Salmaneh, arrived 5. Slow march, walked all the way. General Kennedy gave us tea on arrival. March, fifteen miles.

April 25th. Beautifully cool night, a few drops of rain. Halted, except "B" squadron, who went to Reuben's Tomb, nine miles.

April 26th. Beautifully cool. Drops of rain occasionally. One Brigade Infantry arrived.

April 27th. Cloudy, beautifully cool, drops of rain occasionally.

Extract from the twentieth and last letter I received, dated 27-4-15:—

"We are on the move again, where to will say later, but it is new country to me, and just as flat and uninteresting as the rest so far. The remounts turned ont a very good lot indeed, we got forty-three, should have taken more only short of men, but a draft is coming, we hear. Yesterday was awfully hot, but to-day cloudy, high breeze, and delightful, in two or three weeks (they) say it is awful, but hope then we shall be stationary. We are in camp on a fast flowing river, very muddy and ice cold water. No more news."

[The contents, or to say more correctly, extracts of the contents of my brother's letters to me and his diary are contained in the foregoing pages. It would be superfluous for me to comment on them, beyond expressing the opinion that I think his character can be estimated with no very great difficulty.]

CONCLUSION.

On the 3rd May I received the following telegram from the Depôt 33rd Q. V. O. Light Cavalry: "Regret Major Anderson reported missing 29th April," and on the 5th May I received the two following telegrams, in reply to telegraphic queries I had made:—

(1) "Your brother killed when on reconnaissance; O.C. 33rd Cavalry."

(2) "Military Secretary Chief wires regret Major Anderson killed in action 29th April; Depôt 33rd Cavalry."

On the 6th May I also received this telegram from Simla: "1782/242 Major Anderson, 33rd Cavalry, reported killed 29th April. I much regret the death of your gallant brother, and offer you my sincerest sympathy. Commander-in-Chief." To this last telegram I replied expressing my grateful thanks for His Excellency's kind message.

At the same time my sister received the following two telegrams from the India Office:—

(1) "Regret to state your brother, Major Anderson, 33rd Cavalry, reported from Persian Gulf missing 29th April, further details will be communicated if available."

(2) "Deeply regret to have to inform you that a further telegram has been received from the Persian Gulf reporting that the body of Major Anderson, 33rd Cavalry, was recovered and buried on May first.

"Lord Crewe desires to express sincere sympathy with you in the loss of this gallant officer."

My sister also received this telegram:—

"Buckingham Palace 5th May. The King and Queen deeply regret the loss you and the Army have sustained by the death of your brother in the service of his country, Their Majesties truly sympathize with you in your sorrow. Private Secretary."

This was, of course, duly and most gratefully acknowledged.

From the various accounts which I have received, the short description given below shows from the material at my disposal what took place. On 29th April a cavalry reconnoitring detachment under the command of Major Anderson, 33rd Cavalry, was operating in Arabistan with orders to examine a tract of country on the bank of the Karkeh River. During the course of their reconnaissance, the detachment came across an Arab encampment, the Sheikh of which professed himself friendly, and gave information as to the whereabouts of the Turks. The detachment watered their horses, taking full military precautions, at a place pointed out by the Sheikh. Immediately this was done, however, the Arabs suddenly treacherously attacked our troops. Thereupon Major Anderson ordered his main body to retire at a trot, and recalled the advanced guard and flanking patrols. As soon as the main body began to move, fire was opened by the Arabs from several directions. In the fight which ensued our cavalry inflicted considerable losses on the Arabs, but it is regretted that Major Anderson was killed.

It should be mentioned that Lieut. Bailward, 26th Cavalry, and Lieut. LeMesurier, I.A.R., attached 33rd Cavalry, also were killed in the same action in which my brother lost his life.

The whole cause of the tragic loss of these three noble lives was the gross treachery of the Arabs, and when this is the case one can only accept the inevitable, and view it as the Will of Providence.

The following extract appeared in the *Civil and Military Gazette* of the 12th June 1915.

ARAB TREACHERY

How Lieutenant LeMesurier Died.

Calcutta, June 11.—The following letter, describing the death of Lieutenant LeMesurier, has been written by a brother officer to one of Mr. LeMesurier's relatives in Calcutta. Mr. LeMesurier, who was formerly a member of the Assam Valley Light Horse, joined the Indian Army Reserve of Officers in November last:—

"In going through your brother's papers I discovered that you were his next of kin in India, and I am writing to tell you about the brave fellow's death. I used to know your brother at Wellington, and we often used to talk over school days together. I was not present in the action in which your brother met his death, but I heard all the facts. His Squadron Commander, Major Anderson of my regiment, was also killed at the same time.

"It happened like this: One squadron of the 33rd and one of the 7th were sent out on reconnaissance some 15 miles from camp. They were met by Arabs who pretended to be friendly, and warned them that the Turkish army was only three hours march away and to go back. They went back about one mile and watered their horses and stayed there some time. The rear guard had been told off, and your brother was sent to give them a message to keep much closer to the squadrons. He galloped off, told the troop leader, and started to come back. Just as he turned hostile Arabs, who had been collecting round under the cloak of friendlies, opened fire. More mounted Arabs closed in and your brother was hit and fell off his horse. A native officer and three men were there, but seeing him killed and surrounded by some forty Arabs could not bring his body in. The remainder of the rear-guard were cut up. In the meantime the remainder of the two squadrons were being heavily enfiladed, and were some 1,000 yards away, so were unable to help.

"Next day a strong force of cavalry went out and recovered the bodies. Your brother was buried beside Major Anderson and Lieut. Bailward, at Brackey, some thirty miles from Ahwaz, near Karun River, in Persia."

An officer in the 33rd Cavalry wrote to me as follows :—

"Your brother's body was discovered near his horse, and only about four hundred yards from those of poor Bailward and Le Mesurier. I and some of our men buried your brother, and bathed several gun-shot wounds, any of which would have been sufficient to kill outright. He must have suffered no pain. I feel so sad at having to write you all this."

The trumpeter, No. 2904 Ram Rikh, of my brother's squadron, was with my brother to the last, and badly wounded, and when in hospital was visited by an officer, who relates his interview in the following words:—

"I had an interview with the trumpeter (wounded in hospital) who was with your brother till the last. I think you may safely say Mac was shot practically dead in the trumpeter's arms. First his horse was badly wounded, so he was unable to join his squadron; the trumpeter offered him his horse, but M. refused to take it. Then Mac was shot apparently in the spine, and the trumpeter caught him; the trumpeter was then badly wounded himself, his bridle arm paralysed. His revolver and trumpet in his right hand as well as supporting poor M. and his reins in his teeth, firing was general all round, and his horse took charge and bolted with him. It is all too horrible for words. I know the trumpeter well, a good staunch fellow, and I am sure all he says is true. He is very broke over poor M's death."

General Kennedy in writing to my sister, who had thanked him for all the kindness he had shown my brother when he was seedy writes; "When the Arabs opened fire your brother sent his officers on various errands, and himself remained behind between the main body and the rear guard, in the post of danger. He could by galloping back to the main body almost certainly have saved his life, but this would have been to desert his officers and the rear guard; as was his nature he chose the braver course. In him I have lost one of the best and most reliable and gallant officers in the Brigade."

The following passage appeared in a letter published in the *Civil and Military Gazette* of the 25th June, entitled, "In Mesopotamia: The Trials of an Expedition."

"I was awfully sorry about Major Anderson of the 33rd who died the other day. He was one of the best and a most amusing man. A red tab was to him what a red rag is to a bull. He had been here from the beginning, too."

The writer of the above is unknown to me, but what he says quite coincides with what a friend of mine wrote to me who went to Mesopotamia, after my brother had been killed. He says: "I have heard nothing but expressions of the deepest regret at the loss of one of the best soldiers and best fellows who came on the show. There is no question about the fact, he is universally regretted, as he was respected and admired."

The Persian name of the place where my brother was killed is "Imamzadeh Ali Ibn Hussain."

It is not my intention and I think it would be out of place for me to say more than these few words. My brother and myself had throughout our lives been the greatest of companions, so that his death makes a great blank in my life. He was killed in the service of his King and Country, the death he would have preferred to any other, whilst serving with his own regiment to which he was devoted. He died as he had lived, a true man and a gallant soldier.

"*MORI PRO PATRIA.*"

www.ingramcontent.com/pod-product-compliance
Lightning Source LLC
Chambersburg PA
CBHW052053220426
43663CB00012B/2559